IN THE DO

Since his debut collection, *Death of the Suburb* in 2018, Simon has become a regular performer of his poetry at live events on podcasts (often alongside Justin Moorhouse) and, more recently, on YouTube (with Arthur Smith and Julia Donaldson).

This new collection was written between 2018 and May 2020 and includes commissioned poems for the The Tylers Trust, Steyning 10:10 and Brinsbury College.

Simon works as a tree surgeon and lives in Steyning with his family.

'Simon Zec's poetry is honest, thought provoking and explores the world around him with passion. Both seeing him live and reading his poetry on the page, I find that passion infectious.' **Henry Normal**

In the Downtime

Simon Zec

THE REAL PRESS
www.therealpress.co.uk

Published in 2020 by the Real Press.
www.therealpress.co.uk
© Simon Zec

ISBN (print) 9781912119493
ISBN (ebooks) 9781912119486

Cover illustration by Benita Hibbert (@benithibbert).
Inside front illustration by Rob Winterson (@wintz_art).

For Bean, Kip and Fab.
You continue to inspire and tolerate.

Thanks to Henry for his support, wise words and
tolerating my occasional drunk geeking out

And for Dad.

Contents

Introduction

In the downtime between *Death of the Suburb* – or DOTS as literally one person is calling it – and the release of this, a lot of water has flowed under the bridge.

Elections, Brexit and then a global pandemic. Certainly, plenty of grist to the poetry mill.

This book represents a collection of thoughts on these and other topics. There's very little rhyme or reason to the order and there is no theme to the book. Just, mostly, the good stuff I've spat out in the gaps between life.

During this period, I declared myself Steyning's Poet Laureate. No one else was going to and, consequently, I have taken the role very seriously.

Some organisations and people have asked me to write for them and I have tried to credit them. A sincere thanks to those and their confidence in me.

David is the best independent publisher and I'm grateful for not only his confidence in me but his tolerance of my lack of punctuation.

By some tweet of chance, I have managed to annoy Henry Normal every so often and a big thanks to him for being able to run a few things by him and for the support and time he has kindly given me.

Benita Hibbert (@benithibbert) and Rob Winterson (@wintz_art) have helped me create a book that I'm proud to be able to look at as well as read from. Their original artwork is available as well as plenty of other beautiful work by them.

I was also blessed to have proof reading and support from Henry Everett, without him the book would be spelt worse and would not be half as good.

As I sit and write this, the lockdown lifts and the world looms in a different way. I am grateful for everyone who puts up with my rampant ego and tolerates my whims. Specially the poor souls who I share a house with.

It's an honour to be able to muck about with words and try to put stuff down that helps me work out the world. I do it mainly for me, but I pretentiously pretend that I am trying to do this for the greater good. To be able to create this, my second book *In the Downtime* (or ITD as only I am calling it) just two years after the first one and to continue getting away with it, constantly surprises me.

Who knows what 2022 will bring? Hopefully I'll still be there to write about it.

Love and Peas
Simon, July 2020.

Come find me on:
Facebook: @simonzecpoet
Twitter: @SimonZec23
Instagram: @simonzecpoet

The Treasure Tree

There's a new narrative now
As we define the next era
Covidean times
We are part of tomorrow's history

Trees become treasured
Windows a symbol of primary unity
The pavement a medium for messages
Biology lessons by trees
Stay safe is the new goodbye
The skies clear
The planet given a reprieve
The essential workers look different now
Differences have been put aside
Communities clap and dance
And look out for each other

And fear
And worry
And sickness
And isolation
And death
And waking early
And distance
No hugs

No handshakes
No pubs
No going out

Binary communication
Video calls
Families forced together
Staying in
Saving the health workers
Social sacrifice to save souls
Paid to stay at home
Work redefined

Compost
Loo roll
Flour
Masked people
Daily deaths
Dying alone

And yet
In a wood
Away from the world
An ivy covered tree
Surrounded by dying ashes
Has become a treasure tree
A beacon of hope

Painted stones by children
To show the world they care
Trusting the world to grow it
And let it be

Inspired by the primary school children of Steyning, especially Aimee Light.

In the Downtime

In the downtime
Between fear and grief
There is peace and tranquility
The skies are clear
The planet heals
I forget

In the downtime
I see a pigeon ride an updraft
The green hills
The friendly neighbours
It's not so bad

In the downtime
Words come to me
Nice ones
One's that don't hurt
A beer in a hammock
As we become history
A lesson for generations to come

Our present is the futures past
What did you do in the covid crisis?
I don't know what I'll say
We pulled together

We helped each other
Friends spoke
We found the holes and saw the light in the gaps

In the downtime
The gaps were what kept us going

When this is over, I promise not to forget

When this is over, I promise not to forget
Those that did their utmost
Coordinator, organiser, neighbours and the rest

When this is over, I promise not to forget
The shop keepers and their staff
Who kept going and risking themselves to keep us safe
at home

When this is over, I promise not to forget
How those shops kept us stocked
With flour, compost and loo roll

When this is over, I promise not to forget
The tradesfolk, pubs and restaurants
Who put their business into a coma
To protect us all

When this is over, I promise not to forget
Those who changed their livelihoods
To keep the rest of us going
Learning new tricks and helping out
Just trying to stay afloat

When this is over, I promise not to forget
The sacrifices of the carers
From hospitals to the community
Doing the things we cannot do

When this is over, I promise not to forget
That you're the bastions of our community
The ones who deserve our respect

When this is over, I promise not to forget
The carer, who cleared up my father's mess
And helped get him the help he needed

When this is over, I promise not to forget
The paramedics or the neighbours
Who got him to hospital
And the nurses who held his hand
Comforted the confused old man
Reassured whilst I wait at home
And the doctors who IVed him
Prescribed him back to health
All those people doing what I can't do
Stranded so far away

When this is over, I promise not to forget
All the things that have changed this world
All the people who've tried to save this world
All the people who've just stayed at home

All the teachers who've gone into work
All the politicians who've tried to protect us

When this is over, I promise not to forget

When this is over, I promise not to forget

Broken

I don't care anymore.
Worn down by it all,
Broken and tired,
Drained and disheartened,

Lost the fight,
Given up the battle.
The war was lost
A long time ago

I've been water tortured,
I've been barracked,
I've been hassled,
Resources run dry

Too long I've been fighting,
My limbs needled and pinned,
My bones screaming and aching,
My brain hurting from the strain.

The glass in my hand
Wants to be thrown at the wall,
The plates on the side
Screaming to be smashed on the floor.

The birds in the garden
Scratch at the empty feeders,
The plants in the ground
Grow unfettered and unkempt.

I'll watch the waters rising,
Won't sandbag at the door –
Let the drip alone,
Watch the stain soak into the floor.

Pick again at the scab,
Let it never heal over,
Bite out the splinter,
Let the blood never stop.

I turn from the light,
Close the curtains and eyes,
Leave the heating down low,
Let the cold delve deep.

Brian

Your benevolent drunken generosity .
Bringing poetry to a pub that reluctantly opened its
arms.
You bring tales of flights of realities.
Rhyming stories with a glint in your eye.
Your poems, your performing blossomed as you found
your voice.
Too soon these will be gone.
But your playful spirit infects us all.
May we, once, be too drunk to read.
That last gin that sends us over the edge
And loses our focus.
Will always be a Brian.
May the pub, split between performers and regulars,
Be silenced and unified and hanging on your words,
You are the thread that knits this night together

Countless nights to come

I left you to sleep
As I could hear your breath
Drifting through the dark
I found a bed
Empty for me
To snore restlessly
To take my disturbance
And leave my comfort
To extend your welcome rest
As I toss and turn
In this single bed
As the sun rises for the morn
I'll come to you
With a coffee and smile
As late as I can be
And I'll miss you tonight
But we have forever
With countless nights to come

The epitome of white male privilege

I am the epitome of white male privilege.
I have nothing to offer, apart from the overconfidence
and arrogance of my own thoughts
I stand in front of you with no originality,
No speciality,
No thing to stand me out from the amalgam of
mediocrity that surrounds and dominates.
Why should I be the one to do this?
To give you hope that you too could do the exact same
thing.
To think that my thoughts have enough worth to be
reflected back to you.
With no rhyme,
No rhythm,
No spatial awareness.
And you suck it up,
As I sick it out.
Validating each other.
With no passion.
No emotion.
Like a pointless affair.

The Imp

There's this imp that comes to visit
At the strike of four o'clock
Knocks on the door
Doesn't wait for an answer

This gangly limbed imp
Stretches in through the window
Steps into my house
And waits for me to come

As I walk to the door
He hides in the living room
Waits for me to pass
And climbs onto my back

This gangly limbed imp
Stretches his long bony fingers
With his long pointy nails
Injects himself into my nape

Straight into my veins
To my heart, my blood, my brain
Yearns me to distraction
Pulls me to the cupboard

This gangly limbed imp
Endears me to the glasses
Down to the wine rack
To the bottle opener draw

The glass, the wine, my brain
Unite in imp-ease-ment
To satisfy his urges
Fulfil his earthly cause

This gangly limbed imp
Succumbed, succoured and sated
Slinks off subterraneously
And departs until tomorrow

5th December

Happy birthday, mum
I'm sorry I can't come to visit.
I'm so very busy today
Not sure I'll have a chance to fit you in.

This is probably not the worst I've been to you
I'm sure on the list of disappointments, this one isn't
very high up.
But this one I'm sorry about.

As the years pass my guilt evolves
But it all seems too late.
Too late to apologise.
Too late to make amends.
Too late to do anything.

On the occasion of Henry's 50th

He was repressed and unemotional
A hard nut to hug
Hiding behind his distractions
And enveloped in his layers
Betty Blue was all he could be with.
But at least he was funny.
The most emotional he got was when he cooked his
milky mushrooms.
At parties he was the soul and life,
Brash, engaging,
Definitely never bland.
There was no one else you'd trust at the far end of
the table lining up the buckets.
Always reliable to have the cauldrons prepared.
MISTER E
Cottage man.
Nova man.
The man who always brought David Grace.

But he'd be there when you need him.
And we'd be there for him.
A man who after ten years would finally be ready
for a hug.
But when that hug came.
It meant the world.

And now he's reached a point in his life.

A mid-way.

And after all these years he may actually make it to
100.

It's a miracle he's got this far

And finally he seems able to crack on with the next
half.

He seems complete, content, controlled.

He's the best he's ever been.

The funniest he's ever been.

The happiest he's ever been.

He will always be someone's best man

And he'd always make you the most amazing full
English.

Until he put on your plate those bloody mushrooms.

Sliced and boiled in milk

The worst thing in the world you'd ever tasted.

But apart from that. He's fine.

Commissioned by Mr. Christopher Marks for Mr. Henry Everett's birthday

Glastonbury tickets

I didn't get Glastonbury tickets this year
Thought it best to not bother
I didn't get online at silly o'clock
To be sadly disappointed

My years of consecutively consistent commitment
not appreciated by the conglomerate that is the
Somerset farm converted into a city

So I just didn't bother

I won't get up early to try and bring back the great
old days
I never jumped the fence
Or snuck in
But I know people who did
I never got stuck in the mud
Or soaked to the skin
Or off my chops
But I know people who did

I never actually went
But I know people who did

Oh, glass of red wine

Oh, glass of red
Sweet fruity cold
It's been four weeks
Since we last met.

The imp has chastened
The urges furthered
The mornings eased
The stomach shrunk.

I sit and consider you
And sup you thoughtful
To plan a new path
And see what happens

Re burn

Burn all the last of it
The dregs and the knock offs
Dig up the old stuff
And burn it all up

The off cuts and rotten ones
Covered in bind weed bits
Slugs and the snails
Took over long ago

The summer is waning
Soon it'll be raining
The sunsets turn to mist
And the night's drawing in

They already know

A 16-year-old took a boat halfway round the world
To tell them something,
THEY ALREADY KNOW.

The papers are full of stories of imminent
    destruction
But you know what?
THEY ALREADY KNOW.

Children, across the globe
Went on strike on Fridays.
Inspiring the rest of us
Telling them something,
THEY ALREADY KNOW.

We recycle papers and cans and plastic
And bags and crisps.
Doing all we can to change our world
But they need to do more than us
But that's something,
THEY ALREADY KNOW.

And the next generation,
Making placards
And shouting from the roof tops.

Telling them something,
THEY ALREADY KNOW.

We've been banging our heads against the wall,
Wearing badges.
Singing songs.
Signing petitions.
To tell them something,
THEY ALREADY KNOW.

And those in control,
Get us to do all these things,
Whilst they're:
Fracking;
And oil refining;
And bombing;
And not funding solar panels;
And setting pathetic targets that won't touch the sides.
So we strike.
To tell them something,
THEY ALREADY KNOW.

But we'll keep doing this
And keep doing this
And keep doing this.
Because it's our world
And it's their world
and all of us together,

Are United in single mindedness.

Retirees.
The Middle aged.
Generation Xers.
Millennials.
University students.
School children.
Toddlers.
Babies.
We're telling them something,
THEY ALREADY KNOW.

So we'll keep doing this
And keep shouting about it
And keep protesting
Because one day they'll listen
And one day it'll change
And one day this will be over

And you can't fight us
And you can't stop us
And you can't defeat us
But of course that's something,
THEY ALREADY KNOW.

Barry Harry Stu and Dad

Barry Harry Stu and Dad
Sat in an Indian restaurant
They'd known each other for over 200 years
Seen each other marry, have kids
Watch their kids have kids
Seen their businesses grow and stop
Watched each other bloom and droop.

Barry's never eaten curry in his life
'Take your Immodium' was warning from his wife
'What should I eat?
I'll risk the meat
Something bland with no spice
What do you think will be nice?'

With Harry's wide knowledge of Indian food, Harry
    advised him
You're better off with tikka masala, probably
    chicken.
Harry had just come back from India, you see.
He and Helen were there in November, 4-star hotel,
    I believe.
Travelled around the north, stopped in Kandahar
Amazingly, there's actually six Jews who still live there.

Harry had a vegetable curry and a mild lamb one too.
Went for a paratha, didn't fancy a naan.
Stu doesn't say much, he sits quite quietly.
Studies the menu, then chooses wisely.
Surprisingly, he goes a bit different.
He chooses a butter chicken.
Stu's new partner's daughter has just had a baby
No one knows what to call a non-married 76 year-old's
partner's daughter's child.
The modern world has left them no vocabulary.
It all seems so confusing nowadays.

'What'll you have, Norman?'
'I'll have the tandoori chicken'
'Can you see the menu alright?'
'I always have that, right?'

The food comes, in waves of plates.
They stare and sniff in wonder, these four old mates.
Each dish put in front of their respective place.
The look of fear, on poor Barry's face.

Barry has a taste of his chicken tandoori.
He loves it, it's great, he tells us all with glee.
Harry, wishing to encourage, offers him his plate.
Barry tries them too, thinks they are both great.
Dad shares his chicken.
Barry liked it so much, he went back again.

Stu's butter chicken, goes quietly unshared.
No-one asks to try Stu's, no-one dared.
Stu doesn't like to share his food.
No-one asks to do either, don't want to be rude.

'Don't you like to share, Stu?' I enquire.
The others stare at me, like I've set him on fire.
'It's the quickest and most effective way to transmit
    germs and disease.
I never share a plate of food with anyone, not even
    direct family.'

The silence slowly goes
The chat starts to flow
From Arsenal to trips away
They all have so much to say

Soon it's time for me to go.
To leave my past and escaped future.
I make sure Barry or Harry or Stu will take dad home
And I leave this neon lit, noisy town.

With barely 100 years between us, I go back to my life.
With shared food, spice, my kids and my wife.

I look through the window as I leave
And see these for old men chatting happily.
Finishing off their diet cokes.

Telling the same old jokes.
These four old blokes.
Barry.
Harry.
Stu.
And dad

Don't Mourn For Me

When I'm dead just sing together
Sit round a fire
With strings and harps and drums
And harmonise just for me
I want the mollies
Woodshedders
Make Jeff do a solo
The Chord Welder welding till sunrise

Don't mourn for me
Just sing prettily
Just in harmony
Till sunrise

Thacker plugged and lost
Tim's there with his hat
Maurice Pete and Mick
All sat having a chat

I'll be watching on
With a grin on my face
Happy to know
Beauty will be in its place

Don't mourn for me

Just sing prettily
Just in harmony
Till sunrise

Write me the best song in the world
With solos for everyone
Leave a space for my harp
And imagine I'm good

Nick Graham Thacker
Flakey man in tow
Play one last song
And play till sunrise

Carving a Stone

Just because you've got hair on your legs,
Doesn't make you a man.
Testosterone fuelled anger don't mean you're all
  grown up.
You can try and make sense of this world
But it won't fit together
For one hell of a long time.
Maybe not ever.

Self-control and perspective
Will grow upon your soul
Finding your place
Finding your thing
Finding your happy space
Might take you so long

I'm not sure my advice
Or my take on this shtick
Will make it any easier
I'm not sure you'd listen
Or give half a toss

I'm not saying it's easy
I'm not saying I'm right
But you could hear of my cock ups
And turn left instead of right

I'll show you movies and comedies
And teach you about punching up
But securities and planning passed me by.
I can't tell you how to have a healthy parental
    relationship.
I can't tell you how to be safe
But if you step up to the plate when it all hits the fan,
Then maybe I'll have done my job.

You are me and her and all those before you
But you are your own fair self.
You aren't perfect,
No one is
But you're special and amazing and make me proud.

But the stone you are carving,
Isn't half finished.

An Arbitrary Point

The echoes of the day
Just hanging around
A concept defined by a calendar
An arbitrary point in time

The pain and anger and hatred and confliction and
    sadness and remorse
Ease as the years pass by
A more religious person would light a candle
Let it burn for twenty four hours
Just to have the reminder
But not me

The birds still feed
The kids still need
The trees still grow

This arbitrary point
Just for a day
Puts up an umbrella
And shades me from the world

The Apperiffic Age

You know what?
We're not happy
We've been squeezed
We've been austeretised
We've been priced out of the housing and job market
No housing to inherit
Spent on overpriced care homes
We can see what the other half have
How the top ten percent are instagramming their
    Success
And you wonder why we are angry
And don't rely on the mainstream
Because it says nothing to us about this life
The world is a pre apocalyptic nightmare
In this multi-dimensional superfast broadband apperific
    age
Convention doesn't cut the mustard

So we look to the borders of life
The Yaxley-Lennons, the Farages, the angry young
people shouting at us via YouTube.

These radical solutions to bloodlet our anger and
    our outrage
They shout out to us saying they are on our side

Using us as a way to get your support
We are in this together

We are prime for the picking
We are low hanging fruit
We are ready

Me Me Me Me Me

I'm so vainglorious that when I listen to Saturday Live
I imagine it's me with the amputated leg
Turning my tragedy into a bestselling book
Anecdoting away the pain

How far will I go to fulfil my dream?
I don't think I'd consciously hack my own leg off
But I'd certainly try and remember it all to mine it
at a later date

Unknown

How am I supposed to know
If I'm not happy?
What's my gauge, my understanding?
What is normal?
What is not?
I'm not really sure I know.

The tree's bows are burdened by the fruit.
Pulling itself over,
With the sheer weight of abundance.

Is this just stress?
An accumulation of life
The daily grind
Or does it go deeper?

Grenfell

It's been two weeks since you were all so concerned.
I've become a talking point.
I'm a metaphor now.
I'm a political point.
I'm a poem on Newsnight.
I'm an article to be shared.
You're still aware of me but you've moved on.
I'm just part of the general anger.
This political movement that I helped create.
I couldn't even bring down the government.
But I'm still smouldering.
Still hiding the bodies.
There's still posters up near me.
Faces that are probably unrecognisable now.
Lives destroyed.
Hearts broken, families destroyed.
Gaping aching holes.
In a few weeks only a small part of this world will
     remember me.
But for others I will never be forgotten.
I'm an inferno of a butterfly wing
A murderous sea change.

Garden View

We brought the gold finches into the garden
They brought the greens
Then they brought their young
Sat not six feet away from them
They fed on the sunflower hearts.

They would hide in the birch tree
Then swoop in to feed
Noisily filling themselves up
The countless sparrows diving in and out
Would surround the feeders too
Taking the mixed seed

The proscenium arch of green fills our back garden

My Career

I'm going to be an influencer.
I will influence.
Sponsored vlogs.
Youtubing.
Redditting.
Pinteresting.
Tweeterringing.
Instagrammerising.

People will donate to talk to me.
Not to talk directly, mind.
Via online.
PayPal donation for preferential contact.
My content will relate in its relatability.

Brands will want to be endorsed by my brand.
This will be my career.

The House of Damocles

We planted trees
And fed the birds
Fixed the taps
And mowed the lawn

The promise of longevity
Let us do so many things
But dig much deeper
It's just fickle sand

The ways of the Old Guard

As the way of the liberal is decried
And the rise of the far right climbs.
It feels that it is the last violent throw's
Of the white man's dice.

Our European empires of yesteryear,
Centuries of dominance,
Declining as the world is no longer ours.

This new age.
Of global reach.
Culture is multiple.
Society is international.
Gender is fluid.
Toilets are neutral.

The old guard,
The old ways,
Are being left behind.

And the power doesn't want to be handed over.
It won't change hands without a fight.
To change society you need violent revolution.
As the old guard desperately clings to power.
Lashing out as it drifts away,

So the hegemonic death throws try to beat down the
    tide
Captain America is replaced
Iron Man is no longer
We are Black Panther
Captain Marvel
Multi coloured
Multi cultural
Multi sexual
Multiples

Soon the world will be renewed,
The tiles reshuffled.
The board reordered.
And with this reset,
The world will be good again.

Sunday Morning

The shamboling shaken wreck
Stumbled to collect the car
He was cobbled together with coffee and
    responsibilities
The short-termist fun of a big night
Brings the long turgid terrible tension of hangovers.

Drenched and Cold

The rain drained away the sorrow
Too distracted to concentrate by the enclosing darkness
Each raindrop water torturing the weight off my
    shoulders
Drenched and cold
Dripping and dank
But the day's labour in the downpour
Was more desirable than the impending worry

I want #2

I want to be rich
I want to be minted
I want to not worry at the end of the month
Not be scared of looking at my account
I want smoked salmon
I want rib eye steak
I want to eat take-aways
Whenever the hell that I want

I want the car serviced
I want a big gas guzzling car
I want that new stereo
So I can adjust the volume without fear

I want spoilt kids
I want them to get whatever they want
I want them to have no empathy
With people like me right now

On Discovering one is Fungible

I discovered one Saturday night that I was fungible.
I found out via twitter.
I had to Google what it meant.
Then I put a Facebook update about it.
As soon as it got out there I could feel myself being
    fungibilised.
My twitter followers started to drop.
My Facebook friends started to shrink.
I glanced at the friend suggestions and there was
        some generic Jew looking, middle aged, middle of the
        road poet/tree surgeon staring back at me.
My fungibilimesis.
People started to recommend him for work.
With lots of my old friends saying how good he was.
His poems got broadly ignored on social media, just
    like mine.
Over the coming weeks my work started to dry up.
I ran out of things to write about.
I ran out of things to talk about.
I started to shrink.
My family drifted away.
My fungibilisation was complete.
It was a full fungibilosophosis.
I watch now, from afar, as my fungibilacement lives
    my life.

I catch his eye sometimes.

He looks straight back at me.

He winks, just like I do/did.

But I see what he sees now.

I see what he had gained and I have lost.

But I won't take it lying down.

I'm planning my refungibilisation.

It may take a while.

It may be tough.

But the inherent weakness in us fungiblae is our
    strength.

We are fungibilant.

And I will refungibilise.

And I will be refungibiled.

Punch Up

The low hanging fruit
Are easy to get
But the ones at the top
That take a ladder
Or a white knuckle climb
Are the juicy sweetest ones

The thug at the front
Being manipulated and guided
Is easy to fight
Shout at him
Confront him
But you won't stop the next

Follow the strings
Look to see who guides his fist
Find the forces of darkness
The media and influencers
Propagandarers making their points

The weak or the poor
The vulnerable or powerless
The ones not fitting in or swimming against the tide
Don't need knocking back
Don't need pushing down

Don't need your easy choice

Look up
Stare into the sky
Look behind the clouds
Punch up
Punch hard
And punch deep

3 am

The shard of moon splits the floor in two
As the dark worlds are broken by light
I face them
As the cold of the night
Embraces my heart

Whatever courage we have
Whatever strengths need to be found
We will stand together
We will bind these worlds with love

For the sun will soon rise
And I will face these world's anew
With love and support
From everywhere
And everyone

Commissioned by Tylers Trust (www.tylerstrust.co.uk)

Lost

So many words wasted
So many words lost
Drifted off into the ether
Because I forgot to write them down

The cleverest combination
The sheer unadulterated brilliance
Lost

That first thought of the day
Screaming to be remembered
Telling me to write it down

But I can't be arsed
Or I'm too polite to scribe it
Or too busy to stop

It's just an echo in my mind
A shadow hanging around once the sun has gone

Write!

Write
You must write
You are the start of the future
You are the next generation
These first leaves on the tree
The buds bursting open
To see the world anew
To smash down the walls
And rebuild in new and different dimensions
These works that we've created
These conventions and pretensions
Need your fresh eyes

You See it
You Say it
You Mock it
You Remake it

That first love
That first rush
That first hit
That first kiss
That first sunrise
That first death
That first failure

That first success

They are gone for me
I have to recreate to create
But as you live it
And as you see it
Then your words will be better than mine
Fresher than mine
Newer than mine

So write them
Put them on a screen
In a book
Online
Anywhere

Because one of you will be the next whatever we have
    now
And the sooner you start the greater you will become

It doesn't have to rhyme
It doesn't have to scan
I doesn't have to be anything
It has to be you
From your heart
From your soul
And from your mind

So write
Whenever you see
Stop and jot it down
File it away
Wait for it to call you back
Then spend time with it
Nurture it
Feed it
Throw it away if necessary
But stick with it
For whatever it is
Whatever anyone else says it is
It is beautiful
And it is worthy

For each acorn
Each berry
Each tiny seed on a strawberry
Can become a mighty oak
Or a 5000 year old yew tree
Or a plate of juicy sweet happiness to be consumed with
    joy

You might not succeed on the first attempt
People may not appreciate what you have done
But if, in a room of 60 people
It resonates with one of them
If one person, at the end of the night shakes your hand

Or if it makes you happy
Or solves your problem
Or takes away your pain
Or quietens that voice

Then you've got it
So write
Write!
Write!
Write!

*Written for Brinsbury College Library and Steyning Grammar
School*

I should write

I should write
By a fire
On my own
Wine in a glass
Sun a setting

Long sunny day behind me
Afternoon with friends
Booze and a barbecue
Quiet settled in
Now is the time

I want #1

I want to work in an antique arcade.
Sat, wrapped up warm, electric heaters on.
Writing down each individual thing sold with an
    initial by it.

I want to sit in an art gallery,
Brightly lit,
Reading a book.
Waiting for someone to come in
And I can tell than about each artwork.

I want to work in a second hand book store.
Reading whatever musty book I fancy.
Reluctantly friendly whenever a browser walks in.
I want to be interviewed by the Reverend Richard Coles
    on Saturday live.
My every inanity soaked up.
My every minor story turned into fascinating anecdote.

I want to be on a podcast.
Talking about my grief.
Or my favourite films.
Or why my creative process is so special.

I want to read out a poem

And have it analysed.
And be asked about why I chose this word or that,

I want to be special.
Do something amazing.
Be warm
And smug
And valid.

I want my neighbour's lawn
And their happy children,
Laughing at my jokes,
Respecting me.

For Jeremy Hardy

I thought I was sad when Bowie died
And Prince
But for you, Jeremy Hardy, it stopped me in my tracks.
Your gentle fervency
Your bourgeois anger
Your Fabian socialism
You made us laugh and cry
To not have you in the world
Isn't right
I imagine you weren't religious
But if there is a God
They should send you back to us
But, instead, rest by their side
Where you truly belong.

After Jeremy

I wrote a few lines on the passing of a beloved
    comedian.
His death stopped me in my tracks.
It didn't take long to write.
I'm not sure it's one of my best,
But as I posted it in various places,
It seemed to resonate.
It got more likes and comments than I've had for a
    while
And it mutated into My Ego.
Every person's like and retweet, every lovely
comment took away the pain of his death
And became a Pavlovian thrill of the like.

That poet, that stood in front of the Grenfell
    mourners,
Part of me was amazed at how he managed to break
    down the barriers of poetry and cut to the heart of
    the people.
To expose the soft underbelly of emotions.
Succinctly, sweetly and raw
So powerful
And how was his ego?
Was this just another gig?
Did it help drag his poetry soul up and help his career?

My small effort was miniscule in comparison
But I read into it and found conflict there.

In want to soak up all the power of Saint Columba
and write the poem to solve all poems.
To find the heart of gold.
To pull out Excalibur.
To find that one perfect line.

But I'm not sure if I'm doing it for the right reasons
For you or me?
Maybe a bit of both.
Maybe you need the ego the size of a planet,
To save the world.

I Bloody Love Brexit (Dated)

I bloody love Brexit
It's such a wonderful thing
With its jargon and arguments
It's a divine distraction.

Brokeback backstop
Island of Ireland
No deal, her deal is such an orgasmic ordeal.

Question time has 55 minutes on it.
We can swim in an Olympic size swimming pool of
    single minded obsessive compulsive Brexorder.

We can watch the parties rip themselves asunder trying
    to appease the whole spectrum.
Votes lost.
Votes won
Leaders clinging on.
Leaders not doing enough.
Backbenchers sacrificing themselves for the greater
    good.

Wielding power and influence with the threat of
    destroying their party.

Speaking for the country who voted for this reason
    or that.
Watching democracy fail.

I bloody love it

No one needs to care about anything else
Because no one will notice

The high street is failing
Libraries are going
The fire service has been cut to the point of
    ineffectiveness
The austerity culture has sucked us dry
Homelessness rising
Climate changing
Employment up but wages down
The health service in tatters
Mental health services are running on emergency
    interventions or a quick six-week fix
Police services knifed to the bone

It all just passes us by.
The masses anger can be distracted over this deal or not
We fight over something we know nothing about
It's the perfect scapegoat

As another meaningful test of parliament.

Or another shady deal.

Will they/she/he/this party/that party/the country
survive?

As the hand cart freefalls closer and closer getting
hotter and hotter.

And those in power can stay in power doing who
knows what

Because we watch with our heads in our hands and
ignore Rome burning

A Ghost in my Brain

She was a poster on an information board in
    Sainsbury's.
A thirty year old woman missing since March.
A name,
Two photos,
A brief description.

Christmas has passed,
New Year had gone,
I spent mine in bed feeling rough,
With both my kids safely at home.

She must have had someone caring for her.
Not knowing where she was.
Not knowing how she was.
Spending the holidays worried sick.

Did she run?
Was she taken?
Did she die?
Was she killed?
Did she just up sticks and go somewhere?
Someone must know something.
Does she not want anyone to know?
Was it all so bad that she doesn't care that they don't

know?

So many questions
And I worry that one day it could me.
Giving the police two photos for a poster on an
information board in Sainsbury's.
Leaving a gaping hole in our life.
Uncertainty.
Fear.

It makes me want to swaddle my boys.
Put them in a time capsule so I can carry them in
    my arms 24 hours a day.
I don't want to become a grieving parent.
Waiting in purgatory.
I don't want that.

So I turn away from the poster.
To shield me from her.
But she remains there.
A ghost in my brain.

This Christmas

This Christmas, I'll try to be better.
Better than last year.
Try to cope and be good company.
And to be a better host.

This Christmas I'll try to be soberer.
Soberer than last year.
Try not to be a drunken fool.
And to be a nicer person.

This Christmas I'll just try to be like you.
And follow your example.
If I get to be half as good as you.
I'll be twice as good as me.

Black Friday

I hate black Friday with a vengeance
The blatant commercialism
The vacuous attempt by business to make me spend
    money
The Americanisation of modern capitalism

Plus that coffee machine I want to buy hasn't been
    reduced enough

First they apped the taxis

First they apped the taxis
And I moaned about the decline of the black cabs'
    knowledge and expertise.
But I downloaded the app.
Then they apped the shopping
And I moaned about the death of the high street.
But I downloaded the app.
Then they apped dating
And I moaned about the death of meeting someone
    in a bar.
But I downloaded the app.
Then they apped the takeaways
And I moaned about the use of unventilated
    warehouses to cook the food.
But I downloaded the app
Then they apped the estate agents
And I realised that wasn't such a bad thing after all.

An improper noun

I have become an improper noun
To be shouted at
Exclaimed at in frustration
Demanded for attention
An errand runner
An assistor
A nagger
An annoyer

I was once relevant
An opportunist
A good head of hair
A 30 inch waist
A name

I wash up
I hide in the loo
Lost in my phone
Snoring on the sofa

I am part of a machine
A member of the team

The Millennium Streets

I walked the streets of the millennium
Watching time pass and unfold with each step
As my hair grew and un-receded
My memories returned.

The stores warped as suburban London mutated
    into urban chic
Waiting for gentrification to reclaim the streets
The coffee had come on leaps and bounds
Finding the one thing I'd kept up with.

My addled brain, hazy and dazey back then
Bemused now by the noise and bustle
Oblivious then to the beautiful diversity
Ensconced in our bubble.

Breakfast at the big chef,
BLT pizza from a vanished place,
Woods where Kenny was burnt (twice),
A ramshackle house full of us kids zooming about,
Kidnapping each other,
Friends who watched Friends,
Pub quizzes at the Five Bells.
We had no cares
Only worries if the rope was long enough to escape the

loft in case of emergency
Just ourselves to look out for
Crazy cooking with the guys down the road.

Now we are old and bald
And greying and fading
Ailing and complaining
Our dreams and fears
Ebbing and flowing
Spontaneity so much harder.

But when the shit hits the fan
I'll run over to you
Just like you ran to me
When I needed you
However far we are apart
It's just a text away from a hug
That hug spanning decades
Draining away distance
And filling up my soul.

On Being a Published Poet

I am a PUBLISHED POET!
A PUBLISHED POET!
I should be writing and spreading my words.
I could develop my brand.
I could be pushing my book.
Promoting and creating.
My thoughts could become something that will get me
    out of my job.
I could be providing for my family.
By doing the thing that I love.

No more complaining about my bad back.
Sore hands could become a thing of my past.
I won't have to look out the window in the morning
    and think: do I want to go out in that?
I could drink my coffee and see those dark clouds as
    inspiring.
The wind pushing the trees and find metaphors in
    the leaves.
All these things I should be doing.

And what do I do?
How do I spend most of my spare time?
What awe inspiring,
Ground breaking,

Universal resonating,
Blah blah blah thing,
Do I do?

I'll tell you.
Sliding my finger over a screen to flick a binary ball
    into a binary hole.
Or build an imaginary city.
Buying pointless things for no reason at all.
Or shooting stupid monsters with a dog with a
    powerful hat.
Looking for that elusive floating gun!

I'm a 47-year old child.

A pathetic waste of time.

Poetic Dysmorphia

I am poetically dysmorphic
Crippled by my condition
I have become stuck in a rut
No faith in my words
Hindered by my diagnosis
Held back by my limitations
I can't write my way out of this
Have to break down the walls
I wish I believed this
I may be the opposite
Poetically promorphic
A worse and more tiring condition
I believe I can just write this
Knock out one willy nilly
And it'll be stupendously superb
Life changing and inspiring
Maybe it's somewhere in the middle
Just words, cobbled together
An anodyne page filler
A bland collection of too long words
In all, if I take away the politics
With no anger to cast out
Not even have a clever rhyme
It may all be just a bit bland

Morning has Twittered

As the sun rose over the downs,
The mist dissipating and returning to source,
People emerging from the nocturnal chrysalis.
Kettles boiling.
Loos flushing.
The grinding of coffee beans.

A car warms up and heads off for the day,
The news discussing the same topic it's discussed
    every day.
Every hour,
For the last three years.
Facebook shows us proud parents parading their
    perfect children.
And twitterers tweet endlessly.

Friday Night Friends

My Friday night friends
Who'll be there at the end
Who I smoke with
And joke with
And dance with
And trance with.

You know who you are
Though some of you are far
But my heart still knows
Cos you'll be where I go.
When life gets too hard
Or I've lost my guard
Or someone has gone
Or I just need a song.
I'll call you up
And you'll be there for me
And I for you.
Just give me a call
When it hits the fan
I'll drop everything
And I'll be your man.

Tinnitus

You are my constant companion
My new best friend

My auditory stalker
My otic tormentor
My auricular reminder
My audible enemy
My audile annoyance
My aural scream

Befriend your enemies
Take them under your wing
Well I'll take you to my quiet place
My idyllic hideaway
And I'll rip your sodding head off
And bury you in the ground

Upsetting the Equilibrium

The predestined piles of plates were willfully
    ignored.
The cupboard of cups and mugs and glasses was a
    post-apocalyptic nightmare.
Wine glass lying with mug.
Espresso cup spooning pint glass.
The cutlery draw had had a lovely day at Thorpe Park,
    fell asleep on the way home and was carried
    up without getting changed or brushing its teeth.
The utensils were having an orgy.
Blended and cross breeding.
The discordant dishes shambling behind a door.
The convoluted cupboard was confused and contrary.

The dishwasher, released from its daily fascist
    regime, had an illicit party while its parents went
    away for the weekend.
It looked exactly the same, but it was a little bit too
    clean to convince anyone that nothing had gone on.
Our ordered chaos had been rechaosified.
Into someone else's logic.
Unsettling my equilibrium.
Making me angry.
Why can't they follow my logic?
The system in place was perfectly workable.

Don't change it.
Put it back where it should go.
Your logic has no place in my kitchen.
Stick to it.
Or cock off.

9th September

There's no dutiful call from mum.
Dad won't remember the day.
My morning ablution won't give me a gift of the lie in.

But a coffee in bed,
And trolling cards from the kids,
With booze and mint chocolates,
Lying around doing nothing.

Facebook feed full of good wishes.
Time to write and noodle on guitar.

Little luxuries,
With peace and tranquility,
Make a middle aged man,
Very happy.

One day in the year

One day of the year
December the fifth
The rest of the days are a blur
The only one is this

In eight years passing
Two thousand nine hundred and twelve
Have all been empty
But eight are all that I see

Me

I'm going to finally write a poem about me.

This Poem

I've been writing this poem for years now.
When it started it was this thing of innocence and
    beauty.
I was so proud of it.
It wasn't easy to write.
Kept me up all night.
Needed working on all the time.

I look at it now
And it just annoys me.
I can see all the imperfections in it.
Words not in the right place.
Misspellings and poor grammar.

It seems annoying and simplistic,
The analogies are trite and a bit too hack,
There's no subtlety,
No texture,
Unrelatable and unremarkable.

I want to like it.
I made it, I should be proud of it.
But it niggles me.
Pushes my buttons.
However much I try to rewrite it.

It just won't work.

I want to smash it.
Delete it.
Pick all the letters apart and put them back together
    in a better order.

Every time I reread it.
The shame and anger I feel.
Chips away at my soul.

I feel ashamed at how badly I feel about it.
About all this negativity.
Looking at it makes me angry.
At the way it has turned out.

All that effort,
For a piece of dog turd.

Other people's poems seem so much better.
Funny, clever,
Well constructed.
I love reading theirs.

Sometimes when I look,
I see glimpses of hope,
The occasional nicely placed word.
Half satisfying rhyme.

Clever placement of clever words.

In amongst the feral sewage.
I find a shiny ring.
Something that makes me smile.
A brief moment.
A hiatus.

I often stare at those small parts and think there is
    some hope for it.

Maybe if I extract the good bits,
Mine down deep amongst the festering muck.
Pull out the crystals
And from that, maybe,
Just maybe
A thing of beauty will emerge.

Hopes and dreams to make money as a poet

I'll write short little poems
Brief and ever so trite
Put them on a block of wood
And sell them to overpaid idiots

Tinnitus 2

The radio's on
The telly's on
The screens are on
The kettle's on
The immersion's on
The toothbrush's on
The dishwasher's on
The shower's on

I'm in the room with no noise
Apart from the constant whistling in my ear
The high-pitched-low-level piercing scream
And it's blessed relief

Things I like to do while on holiday

I like to go on holiday
And pretend that I am rich
A wallet full of notes
To be thrown around willy nilly.

Fulfilling the children's every whim
Feeding them rubbish
And letting them feed the slot machines
Like it's a good idea.

I like to browse the shops
Buy hats I'll only wear twice.

I like to ignore the news
Pretend it's not falling apart
Mindlessly ignore all the signs of the apocalypse
And think happy thoughts.

Read a book
Sit around
Write a bit
Eat whenever I want.

Unrecondeconstructed

He was shamelessly unrecondeconstructed.
After years of having his views vaguely kept quiet,
He was buoyed and released to be himself.

Waiting to be groomed by the UKIBNPDL.
Priced out of the labour market.
Not willing to succumb to the every demands of a
    bloated plutocrat.
While the desperate immigrants will.

The *Daily Mail*, with its long history of offensiveness,
Gleefully tries its best to represent and encourage him.
Lighting bonfires under his feet.
Subtly chipping away and verifying all those dark
    thoughts.

The over rich posh elite, Mosley's in waiting.
Waiting for their chance to seize power.
Harnessing their "brethren",
Speechifying to the masses,
Dividing and conquering,
Sending them on to the streets to fight.
To distract us while they land grab.

And he'll be the one getting martyred when it all
    goes wrong.
Abandoned by his upper class brothers.
Hung out to dry.
While the leaders sneak back into the shadows.
Back to the country houses.
Hiding behind electric gates.
Plotting with their minions.

While he rots, next to a bucket in the corner of his cell.
And his flames fanned by the injustice.
To be turned on again when the time is right.

Post Festival

The light-starved patch of grass
Two giant rectangles
Compacted and alcohol stained
From two weeks of festivities
Are all that's left on this field of dreams.

When the rain returns and the sun re-nourishes,
It will catch up with its green brethren,
Slowly defading.
Regaining its life from the life that suffocated it.
Our sleepy town, unaware of the damage we were
doing to these poor blades.

While we danced and played
Laughed and watched
Listened and learnt

For two weeks we could walk home with smiles on
    our faces.
Booze in our bellies.
Seeing things you wouldn't dream would come to visit.

Those award-worthy festival folk,
The months and months of effort,
Long late days,

Planning and planning,
Meetings upon meetings,
Email chains down to their knees.

They worked their socks off:
Booking acts
Making schedules
Manning the bar
Marking tickets
Managing stages
Herding cats

All they got in exchange were lanyards and hoodies,
Abuse from drink-drenched bar queuers,
And the satisfaction of knowing you brought smiles to
    the faces and long-to-be-remembered happy,
    happy days.
And below, as each day went by, the grass took
    more and more abuse.

Drying out, squashed underneath as those first
    week's downpours herded us undercover.
With late, dewy nights to muddy it up.
Hundreds of us jumping up and down, to DJs surely
    too big to play in this tent.
Long sunny days with midday beers spilt.
Glorious memories built on the carnage underfoot.

And then, as quickly as it came, it went.
Leaving the poor patch released and relieved.
As the patch disappears,
All we have left is our thanks for the sacrifice it made.
It was martyred to the most noble of causes.
Our town is eternally grateful.

Strings of Rings

Time passes
One day you are on a bridge
The next you are walking through Brighton with two
kids holding your hands.

Picnic on a hill overlooking the flat lands.
Piss Pot Abbeying.
Blink and you're sat round a fire pit with the neighbours.

In between so much water has passed under that bridge.
Whilst the bridge moved, got rebuilt and now is
    completely changed.
We are the same.
Our hearts combined like the strings of the rings.
Added to and growned.
But flowing together.

Times have been hard
Times have been challenging
Times have been awful

Times have been wonderous
Times have been exhilarating
Times have been bliss

The times have changed
The times have stretched
The wheels have moved around us
But your smile, your gentle voice
And your gentle touch
Are all I need

The Agents of Austerity

The agents of austerity
Have ruined our fair country
Sat in their memoir-dvanced-bought cabin
Protected by their inheritance
Blind to the realities
But do they sleep at night?
Are their spoilt spared soft hands rubbed in guilt?
Or too busy filling in the telegraph quick cross?
They can be wheeled out on state occasions
Giving a loving obituary to someone they vilified
Accepting they were playing a political game

Tell that to the libraries and pot holes
Explain that as we have another operation cancelled
Their gamification has endless ramifications
They just don't get it

To cut everything ideologically.
It all needs reducing
Without a thought for the consequences.
Profitise the police
Pare back the probation
Skim off the top of social services
Schools sliced
Youth services ripped up

And the debt goes down(ish)
And you looked tough
And the middle classes loved you

But years down the line and the ripples of your
ethos is catching up with us
Kids, bored on the streets, no activities, no jobs, no
future
What else are they supposed to do?
You can vilify them in the papers
You turn them into scapegoats
Whilst you sit in your ivory towers
You got off scot free
Hidden away
Or editing your paper
Or executive jobs in industry
But we are living on
We are living in it

You agents of austerity
Have a lot to answer for

Paper Lanterns

Sometimes I think I write to change this world
    around us
Sometimes I think I write to vent my poisonous
    spleen
Sometimes I think I write to impress the woman I love
Sometimes I think I write to give you what you want

Sometimes it rhymes
Sometimes there's rhythm
Sometimes there is
Sometimes there isn't

Sometimes the words are wrong
Sometimes the words are rude
Sometimes the words are pretentious
Sometimes the words get repeated too much

Sometimes the words come out quickly
Sometimes I have to drag them out from a hole in
    the back of my mind
Sometimes I get an idea and milk it until it doesn't
    work anymore
Sometimes if I keep at it and go beyond the realms
    of annoyance it might go all the way round and
    back out the other end and become clever

Sometimes I think I'm Stewart Lee
Sometimes I'm just Pam Ayres

Sometimes these poems will last
Sometimes they're just paper lanterns
Sometimes they resonate
Sometimes they're just junk

.

The Epitome of Heroin Chic

Frail and pale
Tattooed and weak
She was the epitome of heroin chic

Her skin was as white as the blackthorn in April
Her hair as black as the bark
Her eyes were as green as the leaves that have just
    sprung from the bud
And she was a prickly as hell

If you caught her at the wrong point,
She'd get under your skin, dig in and stay there

So, So Sorry

I get a taste for smoke after drinking too much
Pointlessly getting more mucked up
Selfishly single-mindedly stupid

Needing to blow out by blowing up
The excitement of the recent excitement
Lead me down the garden path
Leaving you with all the responsibility

My idiot brain
Again

I'll collapse somewhere quiet
And cogitate my apology
Meekly and humbly hoping for forgiveness

Hungover and dry throated
An old man regretting the stupid teen of the night
before

Occasionally I rhyme

I want you to be a happy young man
Singing your song for as long as you can
I do not know what you'll turn out to be
Will you be lucky and charming and free?

Will it last long or will it be brief
Will you get broken and surrounded by grief
Will you be brave or will you know fear
Will you be angry and drown in your beer?

Surrounded by friends or lost on your own
Will your life be truly your own
Hampered by expectations and pressure
Or will you try to dive into pleasure

Your life is unknown and your future is quantum
Of all paths before you, you cannot be certain

Jew-ish

I'm a Semite
But I'm not very Jewish
Born into the way
But never really in it
I like bagels
I like pickled cucumbers
I'd chose a salt beef sandwich on rye every day
But I don't believe
I don't celebrate
I don't Practice
But I'm defined by it
Not just by me
But by others too
And that's o.k.
Of my many embarrassing parts of my life I've run
qaway from
This one is one I can never escape

I'm not part of the Community
I don't hang out with many Jews
But when I do there's a little bond
A part that unifies us, however small

I have no ties to Israel
I don't agree with what they do

But intrinsically I'm not brave enough to take sides

And my children, despite being born by a non-Jew
In my head a part of them is Jewish too
I won't take them to synagogue
I won't make them pray
But I'll feed them matzos
And bagels
And Mrs Ellswood's Wallys

And we're rebels and outsiders
But we're hiding in plain sight
Not defined by skin colour
Or country
But maybe by a hint of nose
Or curly hair
But I'm aware I'm different
And there's nothing I can do about it

Front row seats at the Dome

I think I'm trying to help you be a better man than me
I'm trying my best to be the best that you can be
To guide you and allow you
To help you and to show you
Without making any mistakes

But it's hard and I'm not perfect
Can't give you everything you need
I want to show how to try your best to try to succeed
Sometimes just trust me
And I'll show you things to find
For every Marvel movie sometimes they'll be Batman
I think that you're trying to help me be a better man
    than me
You're guiding me to show how to be the best dad
    that I can be
My heart fills with pride when I hear you crack a
    joke
Or volunteer for something, you're always filled
    with hope
To sit in the centre front watching the latest Star
    Wars episode

Will always be you and me

Thoughts and Prayers

Thoughts and prayers
Thoughts and prayers
Thoughts and prayers
Won't get you anywhere

Families destroyed
Families destroyed
Families destroyed
By a teenage boy

The trigger pulled
The trigger pulled
The trigger pulled
And nothing we can do

Spring

The wild garlic hit my nose.
The first time since the rain and the wind had
    started to clear.
The sun warmed the boots.

The buds starting to bulge,
The freshest green waiting to slowly burst from the
    brown.

From the sodden grass and claggy mud,
Tips start to break out,
With promises of yellows and reds and blues.

Primroses, true to their name, forerunners for a
    bright future, run the gauntlet,
Hoping a late frost won't do them any harm.

An errant wind-fallen twig gets spotted and snaffled
    by a forward-planning bird,
Prepping for the work ahead.

The starlings gather and murmurate.
Painting monochrome pictures in the sky.

Finally, after months of colds and coughs.

We look up.
To see the light at the end of the winter.
Plan for the warm months.
Dreams of holidays and parties.
Playing in the garden.
Long warm nights.
Sat round fires as the sun sets.
Laughing, singing, chatting.

A Date Circled on an Empty Calendar

I woke up one morning and two years later she's gone
All that's left is a date circled on an empty calendar
I'm haunted by her
I'm in a slow motion horror movie
Being ripped apart and decimated
Not in an hour and a half of efficient scary story telling
In a seven year drudge
And I'm not even the denouement
Barely reached the second act

Ghosts

We are shells
Living separate lives in a busy house
Screened up and lost in their glare

He is on YouTube
He is on Netflix
She is on IPlayer
I'm just playing stupid games

Sliding my fingers over a screen
Moving dots

We are all dopamined up
Addicted
Lost

Our children are orphaned
We mourn our lost children
I am a widower

No one looks up
Swerving over the road
Walking into lampposts
Ignoring everyone
Screens cracked

Phones screwed
Take the day off to wait impatiently for it to be replaced

Upgrades annually to hand over the fluorescent smack
to the next child
Dealing our own children into a life of binary
Shinary
Addicting
Tapping

Selfieing and filtering more and more crap into the ether

Writing poetry on a screen to be written into a book to
    make it look authentic
Predicatatexted mistakes unnoticed until re-read for a
    fourth time

The tide will never turn
No child will put his thumb in the dam
We are lost

We are ghosts
Shiny faced
fat thumbed
obsessed
addicted
online
empties.

Boxing Day

I ground the coffee for longer than normal.
With the dual effect of drowning out the incessant noise
    and the possibility of a massive cardiac arrest from
    caffeine overdose to give me the rest of the Christmas
    period off.
The over loud YouTube clips.
The weather channel.
The kettle boiling and boiling.
The Alzheimered repetitions of a dead wife reminding
    me of my shell of a family.
The recycling bins stuffed to the blue lid.

Apped up to the eyeballs

Our taxis have been apped
Our take-aways have been apped
Our B & B's have been apped

Our books come from a warehouse
Our shopping comes from a warehouse
Our toys come from a warehouse

It all gets delivered quickly and cheaply
It all gets made quickly and cheaply
It all gets consumed quickly and cheaply

No need to leave our house
Or go into town
No need to browse or choose
Or pay a reasonable amount

But when the taxi we've apped gets found out to treat it's
    staff badly and pay so badly that desperate people do
    the work.
But when the take-away we apped gets found out to be
    made in a metal box with no windows on an
    industrial garage just round the corner.
But when the b and b we apped is just some bore's
    bedroom with no standards and no recourse.

And when the town we live in dies
With no banks
No post office
No book shops
No stationers
No off license

Just charity shops
With overpriced tat that we've thrown away
And betting shops
With fixed odds betting terminals addicting the weak
And coffee shop
After coffee shop
After coffee shop

What do we have left?
The kids sit in the park
Wassapping abuse and banter
Or sitting at home youtubing and online gaming
We stare into our phones
iPadding iPlayer in bed
Android cyborgs
Apple addicts

We blindly drift into the unknown
Apped up to the eyeballs

Trying not to be too self obsessed

Pity the poor partners of poets and performers
Silently side-lined supporting as we're surrounded by
    sycophants
Watching as we wistfully wave whimsy and weft
Adrenaline-fuelled ego driven drinking
And self-obsessed silences sitting scratching for
    sentences that shine

Me too

Me too
Me too
Me too
The list grew and grew.
Five simple letters,
Symbolising pain and fear.
That I have never known.

These words inflicted by my kind
Upon women of all ages and all colours and all classes.
People I've known since a child, since a teen, since my
    twenties, since my thirties, since my forties.
And how many others are out there?
Not brave enough.
Not strong enough.
Not wanting to say.

And is my conscience clear?
Can I be brave enough to say?
That maybe when I was drunk and young.
Tried it on too hard?
Would I write the words to say a different me all those
    years ago wouldn't have been so forceful?
I don't know.
Maybe the point of all of you,

Writing #metoo.
It's there to show,
That none of us are innocent
And we should all take responsibility for what our
    society has become.
What men have done.
And how do we move on?
Seeing these damaged human beings,
Finally saying the unsayable.
Damaged by stupid pathetic men.
Like me
Like him
Like all of us
And I'm sorry
My heart droops
At every new #metoo
A friend
A loved one
An acquaintance
With no rhyme or reason
And I feel helpless.

Hid in the Loo

I got home and hid in the loo
A day of dealing with others
Then home to deal with the rest
The warm coldness of porcelain on naked butt
Sucking me in to some mild serenity
Lost in a game on my phone
Protecting me from a tween
And homework
And emails
And tidying
I don't want to be a grown up
Don't want to be responsible
Don't want to shout
Don't want to get frustrated
So I retreat to some sanctification
Flush the chain on an empty bowl
Pretending this wasn't therapy
No biological need to evacuate
Just a mental need to obliterate
And return refreshed
With a little bit of ability to be the best I can be
Back on form
For a bit.

Looking for the Dolphins

Every day I went out and looked for the dolphins.
Staring into the blues and greens and turquoise.
Coffee in hand, camera hanging by my neck.
The peace and quiet of the waves the wind and the birds.
Blocking out the noise of kettles being boiled and papers
    being read.
All that came were white horses and buoys bobbling and
    the ferry, twice a day.
The unreachable bays with rock falls and tantalising
    beaches.

The house was the biggest I'd ever seen,
As expensive as we were poor.
I was at the opposite end of the spectrum,
With the pot of gold way off in the distance.
The rock stars mansion on a campsite
But the dolphins won't come for me.

If I spot one, there will be others
The dolphins don't hang out alone
I'm just one man looking for a pod.

Somewhere out to sea they wait,
Somewhere in the wide horizon,

Beyond the imposing cliffs,
Deep down and around,
They wait.
For me to turn away.
Put my head in my poem.
And return tomorrow to wait again.

Fab

You've brought poetry back to me
Taught me to re-rhyme
And then the words started to flow
Unrelentingly early to rise
Immediately with a kiss and a hug
A furry ball of love and joy

Hardly anything is ever any trouble
When you're happy you're skippy

My Hypocrisy

Your privilege sickens me.
Your god given birth right.
The lucky sperm fertilized the lucky egg.
And gave you the ownership of thousands of acres and a
    life of questionless respect.
A round of applause for getting your hands dirty.
The amazement that you'll lower yourselves to talk to us.
Things any decent normal person would do is
astounding that you might deign to do it.
People fawning over you.
Socially trained and strained to please you.
I hate the way I hate you for no reason but your class.
But I just want you to befriend me.
I want to shove the plum from your mouth right down
    your throat.

Silverstone

Branded brits bedecked in German iconography in an
    act of patriotism
Parading around promoting pollution
Desperately trying to keep the phone charged
Screaming screeching wheels
Beers bought before the afternoon
Lanyarded hierarchy
Smartphone photographs of your kin playing computer
    simulations of racing
A safe space to geek out
Eat meat
Drink beer
Talk cars
Watch cars
Breath cars
Wearing the clothes of sportsmen looking like
    overweight middle aged men
Being spoken to by young fit people white vanned in for
    the weekend to get our email address and send us
    advertising to sell us more shit
These young people who genuinely don't care about why
    we're there, but pretending they:
1. are interested
2. want to speak to us
3. don't want to take their money and just go back to the

hotel

Glamping or camping we all get to queue for the loo
Timing your poo for the best conditions for a loo full of
    people who've eaten meat, chips and drunk beer since
    Thursday.

Tales of seeing Hamilton walk past. For him to scrawl
his hastily drawn signature as they scream his name.
For a glimpse of a multimillion-pound polluting product
of entertainment fly past and cheer.

And then its race day.
Bedding in early with your best spot. Snacked up, beers
    in, comfy chairs with five hours to go
Excitedly talking to everyone with hopes for Hamilton
    the hero
More cars fly past
Then more
Then more
Then it is time to race
Every glimpse of him needs a cheer
And we cheer every lap
Like a petrol pantomime
Booing this year's villain
Celebrating slip ups
Cheering crashes
The parading cars oozing personality

And then pushing against a gate to run across the track
Collecting rubber
Kids shouldered to watch champagne being wasted
Chanting our heroes name again and again
The excitement excels but is soon over for another year
To sit in traffic
From 200 mph to 15
To shower and sleep
And to finally have a nice glass of wine

Steyning Bookshop

The rock and the butterfly, the beating heart of the town
Providing inspiration and imagination to all who care to
    join them.
Tirelessly,
Smilingly,
Unrelentingly.
From first book.
To Gruffalo,
You know that every one of those books has been chosen
    with care.
Poetry to history.
Fi to Sci-Fi.
Curated for one and all.
Radicalism or rationalism.
Escapism or realism.
From high art to a history of the A272.
Sara and Rob are more than just The Bookshop,
They and all who work there have defined this town,
shaped this town, kept this town alive.

Steyning thanks them.
Steyning needs them.
Steyning loves them.

For Gareth and Pete #2

People travelled from all corners of the world to get to
    this edge of the country.
No one, simply no one had an easy journey to get there
Traveling through the night.
Breaking down at the services watching the coach go on
    and leave them stranded.
Arriving from France to get to the coach, to turn up and
    find Elaine had given you the smallest child's tent,
    even though you were the tallest man at the party,
    even taller than Chris.
People drove miles and miles to pick up the bamboo and
    ensure the flags flew and flew and made the weekend.
The people on the coach were the only ones who had it
    easy.
With pastries and pies and parties and naps.
But they arrived late and had to wait for their pizzas.
The cake's journey was long and late but worth every
    hour and mile.
Though it took about one thousandth of its journey time
    to be eaten.
But no one, simply no one's journey was as hard or as
    long as Gareth's and Pete's.
But they got there.
And we all joined them.

Once the fires died and the bales were put to bed on
Friday night the camp fell silent.

The guinea pigs survived the night.

And we all arose to wraps with a different name cos they
were cooked differently.
And posh bacon if you wanted, or no cheese if you were
dieterily intolerant.
And coffee and tea and preparations and expectations.

And the morning flew by and soon we were transformed
from guests into a choir.
And our love lifted us higher until the grooms and the
best people marched down to us hand in hand with
smiles bigger than ours.

And our feet were planted firmly on the ground and we
felt the silence.
And we heard words and lyrics and beauty and love.
And Gareth and Pete only had one thing to say.
And they finally did.

We were guided through the day by the funniest
accountant to ever host a wedding.
And it all flowed like the fizz of the toasts with cork after
cork popping and pouring keeping us filled for the
toasts and the wondrous speeches.

Then Elton bloody John turned up to perform.

Then snoozed and prepared we all mooched to the top

And the pixies mixed with mattresses and jokes that
shouldn't work and songs of killings and crisis's and
jazz harmonica, hosted shockingly appropriately by
the second tallest man in the field.

And Gareth and Pete stared into each other's eyes with
smiles and intensity as they danced their first dance
as husbands.

And then we partied.
Ronald McDonald mixed with men dressed as women
and women dressed as flamingos and the tallest
Pocahontas you'd ever seen.
With hair and bauble coated coats
And paint bombed children
And outrageous t shirts about Adam and Steve.

Music and fires and burgers and candle lit flags.
And then jellyfish turned up followed by the police.
Three fires burned into the night till not a single bit of
kindling was left.

That night the bales were allowed to stay up all night
and watch the shooting stars.

Again, in the morning, the wraps were wrapped
    differently and named something else
And the cake was cut and gone in 13 seconds.
And each hand-crafted figure was an exact copy of each
    of the guests dressed so sartorial and risky.

To a beach with a second splendiforous picnic and cold
    cold water
And hugs and love.
And then we parted
To start posting on a passed events page to keep it living
    on.

It was said many a time it was the best day ever.
That it has ruined weddings for ever more.
To top it you need to be married under water.

And in the cold light of day as the hang over goes and
    tears sparkle in my eyes as I think about it, I joked it
    was in my top eight days ever.
That was cruel and unfair.

I put it in my top four.

The Real Press

If you enjoyed this book, take a look at the other books we have on our list at www.therealpress.co.uk

Including the new Armada novel with a difference, *Tearagh't*, by the maverick psychologist Craig Newnes.

Or the medieval thriller, *Regicide*, by David Boyle, and introducing Peter Abelard as the great detective...

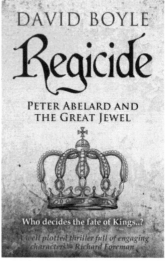